Missile
Hymnal
Amulet

_____

G. F. Boyer

FUTURECYCLE PRESS
www.futurecycle.org

Cover image from the public domain; author photo by Dana Seidl; cover and interior book design by Diane Kistner; Georgia text and titling

Library of Congress Control Number: 2018954442

Published by FutureCycle Press
Athens, Georgia, USA

ISBN 978-1-942371-63-2

For Dana

Church ain't over till the snakes are back in the bag.

—Willem Dafoe, in *Out of the Furnace*
(screenplay by Scott Cooper and Brad Ingelsby)

Contents

i.

_____

ii.

_____

iii.

_____

i.

My Mother Would Be a Physicist

after Robert Duncan

My mother would be a physicist,
and I, her mute neutrino barreling
bleak subatomic winters, whistling
between the bodies of others.

My mother would be a physicist
and would send me forth beaming
in a deep inelastic scattering
to form a new architecture of stars.

Be a fast traveler, be single-minded,
she says. *That is your charm and beauty.*
But my truth is to come between
and between and between.

For mine is a weak interaction,
mine is an elementary charge,
even as I slice through matter's butter,
slip bitterly between strangers.

Sunday Schooling

After church, we threw stones.
I aimed at beehives
under yellow plums

dangling in bland heat, whence
an angry cloud issued forth
to tangle

in my clothes and hair, because,
like God,
they knew me.

My distant self
watched from outside that burgeoning hurt,
astounded

at such precision,
such prompt and fierce instruction.
Oh

forgive me. From that day on,

I trembled
at your malevolent song, the venom
of your rebuke.

Spotted Deer

Lighters click. Cigarettes flare.
Hellfire fills the van.

    All but Dad pop beers

and windows, plug the spotlight in.
My brothers and I gag, slump in back.

Even crewcut, Uncle Larry's hot.
Then there's Uncle Vaughn:

    hillbilly, drunk.

His head puckers like a skinned piglet
when he laughs.

He swigs his beer.
Dad and Larry talk of points,

    suspended hocks, the drain of blood,

their favorite cuts, divvying packs of meat.
From our idling van,

the spotlight sweeps woods and weeds,
stops, mesmerized by eyes.

    We stare out; these other kin stare in.

Crickets ratchet the wild night tighter.
The gun rack rattles. The jackknife springs.

The Fish in the Well

When she was five
my mother dropped

a live fish in a well
then leaned over

to watch it loop
and sink and circle.

The water's mirror
reflected only

her own tousled head
when over weeks

she'd check back
for a ripple, a splash.

At eighty-three,
she tells me she's ashamed

of what she did to that fish.
We sit in silence.

At the bottom of time's
echoing shaft,

our thoughts rise
and circle and disappear.

Fledgling

Springtime. You came home late again.
A cheddar moon on the point of a pine.

Frogs cranked out their vocables against
an undertone of crickets in looming forest.

Dogwood blossoms on open palms.
Your mother, acting calm, asked

some questions—who knows what.
You couldn't answer.

Your father quiet as usual,
sad. You with your itch to be gone.

In the morning, hummingbirds
sipped sugar water

from a plastic Shasta bottle.
You slammed the porch door on your way out,

your head instantly haloed by gnats.
The deaf hunting dog still asleep on the mat.

A Toast

> *Go to the ant, thou sluggard; consider her ways,*
> *and be wise. —Proverbs 6:6*

Here's to the ants
my mother blanched

with boiling water
from a teakettle,

pouring it in
their meticulous hill

beside the sidewalk
in Beaverdale.

Thou laggard, thou dullard,
lift now thy boiling toast

to the spotless counters,
to the threatened *Don't start!*

to the dogs shotgunned
to save on a vet.

Fundamentals: Church of Christ, 1970

Sister Edna placed unsalted matzo
on a paper-doilied plate.

Sister Helen poured our Welch's grape
in tiny glasses

borne in the holes of a silver tray.

Sister Mavis washed them after—
bleeding the sudsy water red.

Outside, on the sidewalk,
the unsaved trod,

indifferent to our special place
in the indifferent heart of God.

Luncheon on the Grass

Discontent with the crumbs of your table,
I inspect pine needles.

Once a cylinder, these have split
lengthwise into three parts.

That's how bayonets are made, you say.
The wound is triangular
and doesn't heal easily.

What are we?
What do we imagine ourselves to be?
Take the knife, slice the apple,
school me in warfare and love.

Lull

Heat drips from the horns.
The garden's out of gas.

In the stupefaction only
fleas leap across

a sweep of parched grass.
Through the screen

their sedative drone...

Today, who could move,
who could care

about the coming storm.
Who could give a damn?

Aerial View of Seattle, August 1963

This is the lake
where the logs float.

These are the mountains
above the town, where buzz saws
brought the old trees down.

And, here, the river
that carried the trees
stripped of their branches
down to the sea.

These are the lakes, the sea, and the sound
that meet as one,
and from here the logs
look like grains of rice
and hardly even matter.

This is the town
arranged in rows.
Houses face the sound or the lake,
and waves reflect the plane in the sky.
Everywhere beauty is in the eye,
and everywhere we behold it.

This is the photograph
snapped from a plane
to freeze the logs as they float
on the lake, to freeze the houses
arranged in rows, the mountains rising
above the town, the river
that throbs like a vein to the sound,
to freeze the light on the grains of rice
and the trees, the trees, the trees.

Professor

I walk across the campus,
amazed again at the reprieve of spring.
The sweeping blades of sprinklers
chop sunlight into colors.

Professor, analyzer, walking talking head—

explain to the class,
for example,
the apricot bloom—

go on, we're waiting—or

how in Brazil
a "surgeon" could pull
the blade from his arm—
no wound, no blood—

or solve

how water
closes again over the entry
of a stone, the surface remembering
itself, keeping its secrets.

A Short History IV

Years passed. We built an edifice of glass.
Monumental, scalded, scaled,
not the least bit cracked. But
we watched, mesmerized, as it broke in half,
our hearts hollow, frozen, tidy—
shot through with ribbons of blood.
Nothing remained
that a modest breeze couldn't collapse.

Snared

A dew-beaded web,
laced among weeds:

in every drop
your refracted face gleamed.

What could have unsnagged you?
You thought you knew.

Yet each year, more color
drained from October,

and you couldn't look. No,
you couldn't look—

even as the spider
sped toward you.

Final Deployment

We're not going to unbury him, are we?
Because we didn't find the WWII uniform

until after the funeral (box labeled DVDs,
laundry room shelf)? Why question

at this late hour our choice of "Dad"
T-shirt and his favorite flannel?

Are we ordering him to the front, *mach schnell*?
Are we disturbing his sleep to murmur,

like some Berliner fräulein,
Was willst du haben into his peaceable ear?

Infinite Loop

Time's old conveyor belt hauls
your carcass-laden soul

into a ripening future—too soon
to harvest, too late to uproot.

Under a cold and withering sun,
bedsheets flap on a line

like doorways to hidden rooms.
And look—there's your mom:

clothespins in her pursed lips,
a laundry basket at her hip,

her feet planted in the grass,
among the rotten pears.

Fable

We ate cherries from a blue bowl
while tendrils of ivy twisted
through the bedroom window.

Nothing stirred but the cats
as they came and went. Outside,
tomatoes slumped to earth in leggy weight.

A brutal wind rose
and the heater sighed like a woman
as we railed and wept in our crystal cage.

And we skimmed the air
like birds asleep in flight—
each with one eye open, only half aware.

My Last Failure

At Forest Park, a nurse
brings meds in pudding

and a blood pressure cuff
amid the blather of TVs.

Now that Mom doesn't know
who I am, I think she might love me.

I remember the set of her mouth
when I displeased her—

the slap, the sting, the lash.
Her eyes' gray flash.

I stayed outside as long as I could
to avoid her anger, always poised

to strike at my first failure.
And I'm failing still—

to spend enough time with her,
to get her out of here.

Like the scraped plates
of poverty,

I am empty.
Like a scorpion, I am barbed.

In Dad's Old Negatives

my ghostly brothers
pose in striped T-shirts,

awkward white-framed
spectacles. Arterial white

trees loom, a circulatory
system of memory.

At the kitchen table,
three kids, birthday, four

black candles.
Me, forking dark cake

into my mouth's fiery cave.

Animals

Minks ran frenzied in their cages.
It was summer, and the neighbor's son,
Junior, had big hands.

The pond hidden in weeds
brewed bog and sumac
and jellied tadpoles.

       Junior said
he'd help me pee,
calloused hands on my legs,

kneeling and grinning and watching
me squat as my pale stream
splashed the ground.

Under a lid of clouds and hissing rain,
tadpoles bloomed into frogs.
I don't know why I thought

of the mink skins I'd seen tacked
to boards in his cellar, or why
I think of them now.

Salvation

The preacher's breath reeked
as he held me close and pinched
a washcloth over my nose.

I did not long to be drowned
for the Lamb. I did it because
I was thirteen.

Oh Happy Day, they sang, they sang,
as I went under and the brimming
river stoppered my ears.

In rubber hip boots,
the baptist labored to raise me
from that watery grave,

but rise I did,
my wet clothes a new skin.
And I turned my lying face to the world.

ii.

The Ideal Poem

The page's whiteness suggests
dirtying, suggests bird tracks or cigarette ash
or piss on snow.

The poem's polite. It doesn't press.
Air and light conspire to spark
a signal flare.

Smoke spirals upward
from chimney, sage, cigarette.
And yet the poem maintains the right

to remain silent as an urn of ashes.
Back doors creak ajar, revealing
the tremor of oyster flesh:

the nursing home,
the wounded deer, the shattered glass.
Click here to submit.

Dutch Tulip Bubble, 1636-37

For six thousand florins, the *Semper Augustus*
we kept in a bank vault.

I didn't open my mouth
then to him.

But after cutting bread and cheese,
pouring wine into a blue glass—the sun

a tipping pitcher—in the fields
ten thousand red mouths did open,

shouting *ruin, ruin, ruin* at the striated sky.

Some Nights

I dream of you at the lake, rowing
toward shore. Horses under a tree

in the new moon's dark.
A hundred love songs on the radio,

the car door standing open.
It begins to rain: silver rain.

Your coat pockets heavy with coins. You
disappear where the horses breathe,

your eyes shadowed in the cricket-filled night.
No one else at the lake.

Rain begins, ghost notes on the cabin roof,
the silver ping on a canoe. Wind

pushes waves toward shore. Some nights
you appear. Some nights I dream.

On the car radio, a hundred love songs play.
Two horses under a tree. A new moon

hangs, invisible. Silver coins droop,
heavy in the hem of your coat.

Nursing

Mom thinks I'm her sister.
Of course I am. These days,
I'll be anyone she needs.

Her lunch tray's abandoned—
bread drying to shells,
yellowed mashed potatoes.

Let us sit and read
Good Housekeeping, or watch
the Waltons on TV, while

she spoons vanilla pudding
into her hairbrush, intent
as if she were diapering a baby.

Peaches

So ripe, the juice
runs luscious down our skins.

Ripe and rot: two sides
of the same hard pit.

Sweet we are, smooth,
with merely a dimple

you can't remove.
No scalpel cut, no satin

stitch, no open leaf,
no seed, no split.

Just blight—
a pucker at the stem

where something pumped
the lethal ripeness in.

Other

My arms around your pillow,
a hard frost.
By tomorrow I'll be down
to the green tomatoes,
the ice-licked apples.
Even Guilt, my other
two-timing lover,
will snort in disgust and turn over.

Driving Lesson

When you bent to pull
the still-warm body
from under the tire,
all that showed
was a smear of blood,
open mouth, soft nose.

Seven steps
up to the front porch
(potted plants,
wicker chairs,
porch swing).

She peered
through the screen,
drying her hands on an apron,
then over her arm
she draped the limp kitten,
like a lesson in nerve
or a lesson in ambition.

The Question

Will we wake up years from now and wonder why?
There's such dog-hopefulness in your eyes.
I have a headache and you shouldn't ask. Yes.

You rub Vaseline into your skin.
The black cat lounges beside the wandering Jew.
I have no hope for this or any love.

Instead, I bring you indifference and flannel pajamas
from the Goodwill store. Wear them and stay.
You will look more beautiful walking away.

Love's Last Feed

Cold spring, moldy summer, chill fall.
You upstairs in your sorry bed,
ruminant.

No fight left in me,
no hay for the goats.
The field pounded dry year after year,
a stone acre.

Let go.
Let me be gone.
Nothing for the goats
but salt and stones.

Living Color

Because you have more rods or cones than I,
could your eggplant equal my ecru? For you,
do flamingos stretch their long cerulean necks?
It could be true. Your seven million cones
put my five mil to shame. Your green could be
my blue. The marvelous spatuletail hummingbird
of Peru darts through a jungle canopy, flashing
rose for bronze, saffron for blue. For all I know,
a chartreuse sun might rise for you in a clear
citrine sky. Undersea, against a reef, the orange
elephant-ear sponge might glow green,
and somewhere, over the strangest rainbow,
a teal and cyan skunk might waddle across
a maroon lawn, unspied by eerie cerise eyes.

Listen

...a bird of the air shall carry the voice
—*Ecclesiastes 10:20*

In the curves
of a transatlantic cable,
sea anemones shelter.

Pigeons roost
beneath a freeway bridge,
asleep to the overhead rumble.

I'll accommodate, too,
grow used to silent evenings,
meals apart,

the cries of geese
down the flyway.
For weeks their silver ribbons

turned like Möbius strips, sun
burnishing their bellies.
You left, too, compelled.

And I, compelled to watch you
through a glass darkly.
Glass—a liquid that shatters,

they say. But really,
it's a solid that breaks.

My Wicked Little Stranger

Drizzle blurred
the school bus windows

as we stopped
in gray predawn.

She mounted the steps,
edged down the aisle

to find a seat.
Her heavy coat

brushed mocking kids
who recoiled

in loud disgust,
held their noses,

oinked like pigs.
The bus pulled out,

wipers ticktocking,
and I stared

through rivulets of rain
as she sat down

beside me. I never turned,
I never met—why?—

the blackened cornfields
of her eyes.

Lost Heart Pond

It draws you in again when heat
drips waxen down
the face of afternoon. The small of the back.

The milkweed touch of air.
When you lie down, your tongue fills up the room.
In any language, the news

is just as bad. Even so, you want to see
what happens next,
as if you're sitting in a dusty theater

while outside spring extrudes another leaf.
The pond shimmers
with dragonflies and striders

among the rushes and weeds. In a dream,
you stir it with a stick, then sink
into its iridescent depths,

because you know
your brother was pulled down, and your sister
also walks the footpath along

that softening edge where something
swims just underneath the surface
like a cottonmouth.

Half-Life

You scratch your feet
for hours, coaxing
shy blood.

      Blisters
map your progress
from ankle to instep to toe.

      Branches
of a diseased elm
at the night window.

—

They tuck you into a steel sleeping bag,
ease a laser eye down your throat.

You don't call, so I make soup.

An offering.

—

In the midnight waiting room,
imagining the soul as a wafer,
pod split and half-unshelled.

Here in this house of souls,
I remember our skin
sweating together.

—

Prayers like smoke.
Can they penetrate, sidle
between molecules
to some hovering god?

—

Roses, havens for bacteria,
I carry out of your hospital room.
Away also with babies' breath
and homicidal ferns.

Under the car door,
one lethal petal in
the dust.

Silo and Barn

Blackened corncobs floated
at the bottom. Last year's corn gone.
Now a scummed wash of rain.

You stuck your head
through a loading window
to look down.

Like a dark mushroom, its shadow
sprang into the square of light
sliding across black water.

—

All the long summer, you chewed oats
from the barn's wooden bins,
resigned and methodical as a cow.

Noise made cows give blood in their milk,
made chickens tuck a secret blossom
of blood into each egg.

Cracked,
that red and golden world
slid onto your plate.

Lost Things Found

with a bow to Elizabeth Bishop

Lunch money still tied in its red hanky.
Plastic dime store ring with peeling silver.
Bangs I trimmed at six.

Rock collection: mica, quartz, feldspar,
lump of anthracite. And books:
the kids who lived with ants,

the girl who got sick from wearing silk
instead of wool in winter.
Here, the cats who made the trip

to the pound, puking in the car
while we kids cried: Fat Orange, Wisdom.
Dusty who went AWOL searching

for lost kittens in the woods
(or so they said). Penuche, who escaped
the car, the vet, his life in one clean leap.

Rabbit drowned in silo murk. Butterflies:
small whites, monarchs
shriveled in jars in the garage.

Young father in his burlap-walled darkroom.
Young mother carrying a pan of beans
across a summer field, cotton dress

blowing against her knees. And here,
the things I felt before I became
someone who laughs at all I say.

Obsession

End-of-summer dust
vibrates in the chicken coop,
chickens long since replaced by dolls.
Whitewash on my fingers,
feathers stuck in wire mesh.
Years later, still that smell.

—

Another dream of water. Which
remains whole through every division.

—

She said we were going to make history,
we heirs of malfunction.
Possibly a drop of water from her wet hair
had fallen onto her lip, her full mouth.
I couldn't argue with her skin,
her long fingers. The smile set
on my face—a doll's—as I drove
afterward down a back street.

—

The streetlights never lit that night,
unnecessary, long-stemmed redundancies
in her luminous heat.

—

Pigeons mutter from the roof.
A brown-headed woman walks underneath.
That's me. I'm the one who arranges

November in a quart jar—lilies in rude poses,
shameless pistils and stamens.

—

The night, not black but red,
curdles with dust as blessed rain begins.

The Disposition

Now we choose
what to do with it

(fluid, flames,
velvet, satin,
concrete vault)—

our father, who

still art not,
no matter what we choose:

walnut, cedar, oak,
mahogany,
pine—

What You've Missed So Far

Dot-dot-dash of thunderstorm
pocking Lost Heart Pond.

Water on Mars.
Raking the damn leaves again.

Scientists say loneliness is a disease.

Sun-charred grass.
Demise of your thirty-year L.L.Bean pants.

A Thai woman feeds herself to crocodiles.
The laughing crows.

Then there's me, finally daring
to remember your waning breath,

the quiet after—

How It Will Come

Like flat stones skipped across a pond:
swift, glinting.

Scattered, a calamity,
a chastisement, a milkweed seed.

Like the dung beetle,
turd-obsessed, cherishing the worst, the waste.

Or the falcon, who believes the hood is night.

Like me, perfectly formed,
held inside my mother, drifting toward the world,

toward long blue shadows over frozen snow
on the year's coldest morning.

Like my foolish self: bumbling, haggard, worn,
full of hope, helpless.

Like a guided missile out of fog.
Like the silence of a silent, silent god.

Venus, Cupid, Folly, and Time

In my dream I brought you armloads of white flowers,
an offering of blossoms big and self-assured,
petals thick and waxy against formal green leaves.

On the third day, the sun rose again. We had lunch
on the reservoir rocks, oddly private
in the middle of things. You told me about a woman

who talked to the moon, sitting on stones
gathering frost in the garden. If she had turned,
she might have seen her house burning behind her.

iii.

_____

Our Father's Garden

We were born in his tangled light and shade,
covered our nakedness in the gloom

of Kentucky Wonder pole beans.
Hairy leaves scratched our skin. Lettuce

and carrots burst warm from the ground.
Dirt on our hands, bugs in our teeth, we bit

into ripe tomatoes, spewed seeds.
At the dump's edge, in the rhubarb and vines,

the serpent dangled from a branch.
Down where the garden met the pasture,

we walked on Sundays, after the blear
of church. Umbrellas of mayapples

grew there, and the blasphemous
jack-in-the-pulpit. There we lounged

on house-sized rocks, climbed the leaning oak
like a stair, quavered at Indian pipes'

blanched light. How blind we were, how
unaware, as the angel raised his flaming sword.

Mercy

There would have been snow
on the pigpen roof, the barn,
the road's frozen ruts,

the collapsing hay wagon.
Dad would've shouldered his
thirty-ought-six, headed out

toward the sound of a stray
with a trap-mangled paw,
sure to be chewed to a stump.

Snow would've covered
the junked car's rotting upholstery—
an offering, a kind of altar.

Sharing an Artichoke

for S. G.

You boil the little armadillo.
We watch the water bubbling
from clear to green, then slice

in half—oh, fearful symmetry!
Such terrifying design, bristling
with a painful vanity—

who would have thought it edible?
We unfold it leaf by leaf,
dip each in lemon butter,

scrape it clean across our teeth.
Layer by layer, we near the center—
the delectable, devouring heart.

Our Lady of the Midnight Kitchen

Beans float like baby Jesuses in the soup.
I get a call from a lost one-eyed cousin.
He says the world is big enough in one place.

I was sleeping in a cold room when the sun came up.
Eyes open, mouth bloody, full of cat-claw
and nettle. Always life unravels like a basted hem.

We go home the long way—wind, sharpness
of new rain, street sinking into my shoes.
Sky of broken glass, of lead, of coal. At night

I gather all my missing pieces, wait for dawn.
The cat hauls his fat body up
to lie like a sack of diamonds at our feet.

Elsewhere

There's a very small planet next to the moon.
Of course we know it's not really beside the moon.

And not really small.

You say it's Mars, who's angry and red.
To me it's just another star.

Day after day, I am tired of slicing the same tomatoes.

Tall elms lose leaves in the wind,
upper branches sparsing out to skeleton.

It happens slowly so we may bear it.

When an ambulance passes, neighborhood dogs
break into disconsolate song.

This is a dry planet. Red dust shakes out

in desert wind—a cold wind with green eyes
like the black half-tailed cat. The sky flattens.

I am a woman of gargantuan proportions, running.

Afternoon Nap in a Pasture

In tall dreaming grasses far
from the highway, sky a speckled

grackle's egg, in languorous daisies,
in the clamor of wild iris and red clover,

you begin to rouse, your eggshell
of sleep cracking, dissolving, and then,

overhead, there they are: a flowering
of cows, a daisy chain, staring down,

solemn and genial circle—dark-lashed,
chewing, bewildered—and your eyes,

too, are a mirror as above them
storm clouds tumble and darken.

Finding Water

Elms shoulder up sidewalks,
dowse underground streams
in clay and metal pipe.

Hair-roots insinuate,
carve apertures, atom by atom,
inevitable, innocent.

As pipes burst their seams,
joints rupture. Larger roots
muscle in while the smallest

savor their new climate—
humid, tropical—testimony
to the power of raw persistence.

The Virgin Queen

She leaves the hive, trailed by drones
who vie to be the chosen one:
to win, then die.

Like some Kama Sutra feat,
the queen and drone meet and merge midair,

forward, backward,
upside down,
at two hundred feet.

Stolid worker bees get back to work on their
obsessive math,

constructing hexagons of wax,
carrying water, pollen baskets on their shins,

stuffed satchels fringed
with blossom dust.

And a plum tree's sweating globes grow fat

and fall, to burst with sugar
near the spent drone's withered shell.

Lifted Up

In a homemade pink dress,
in our usual pew, I drew all I saw:

Dad preaching
with his glasses upside down,

ladies' beads and feathered hats,
a surround of Sunday finery.

We sat for a brimstone-
ridden while, then stood to sing.

Did the muggy drear part briefly?
Were the sheaves brought in?

No. Instead,

    the room
    dimmed, sparks
    of light swam
    into blackening view—

I came to on cool wood,
weightless, a wounded flamingo.

The faces, God's people,
floated above, staring down

in innocence and sin.

HeLa Cells

A cervical cancer cell line derived
from Henrietta Lacks, who died in 1951

Like the homeless, you are everywhere.

Like the boy with five barley loaves and two fishes,
you have fed a multitude.

Like painters on the Golden Gate Bridge,
you reached the end and began again.

Monarch

In a jelly jar
behind cans of primer,

he resides in a murky cellar window,
biding his time,

a dutiful chewer of milkweed leaves
to power his silk factory.

Absorbed in his summer project,
he packs his scrub-brush body

into a green cabinet suspended
             from a stalk.

—

Late summer
he shoulders free: wet, frail,

the orange-and-black wings
pleated, momentarily

halted, to stiffen and pulse,
then capture a current and lift

          matter-of-factly
into the afterlife.

Heat Diary

You know the story's ending—
almost everyone has died—and now

all night teeth rumba in your head.

Night's soggy creak, the glaring
Circle K sign, a star of Bethlehem.

Go ahead, wish again
for rain—the wash, the drain, the gutter.

Write your cosmic address:

city, country, planet, galaxy.
This is your universe.

Then turn over the day, a page already written.

Graveyard Found on Moon

—The National Enquirer

From here, Earth's a sight:
silly beach ball in an echoing tub.

First came life: a series
of straight-backed chairs.
Then we were stuck here
like cloves to an orange,
hung at the back of God's
hall closet,

        entombed
in an eclipsing cheese
where no wind chews
the chiseling from our stones.

Dawn comes round, lucid flange
burning a curve of bone. The sun's a sneer.
Earth's a rare disease, but
we've been cured.

All My Smoky Aunts

Blue smoke sashayed from Camels.
My mother whisked away ashtrays,
cranked the windows out.

Summer heat powdered the garden—
curled tomato leaves crawling with beetles
we'd drown in cans of kerosene.

We ate corn chowder late summer nights.
I envied my aunts' smoky sunburned skin,
that wheatsack lizard birdleg skin,

their husky voices in cigarette murk—
a lunatic stew of abandon and risk.
I eagerly took up my spoon.

Cornfield Math

Reminded of ourselves,
mirrors of each other,
we multiply and divide.

We stand tall above soybeans
near the neighbor's field.
The clouds bring down our snow.

Through the stripped trees,
the wind grows colder.
Now we are seeds,

waiting, half alive.

Now we are seeds.
The wind grows warmer
through the budding trees.

The clouds bring down our rain.
Near the neighbor's field,
we stand tall above soybeans.

We multiply and divide—
mirrors of each other,
reminded of ourselves.

Points of Intersection

The geese leave in October,
a wavering triangle following memory
in feather, wingbeat, bone.

        Where to go
on this gray morning?
Clouds polish a gritty sky, and wind

sweeps through blue trees at water's edge
where brown leaves float across
a tentative geometry of geese.

Blind Staggers

At the edge of vision,
curved like the arc of earth,

light fractures—
an incandescent world of glass

where cold pulls aside
the curtain of mind,

claws crack roots, trees
plummet down, dogs pull bones

from the ground. A horse walks
swaying through a paddock.

Singing scallops pop their shells
in the chew and clutch of tides.

Aluminum hearts and ankles break.
A calyx of sassafras.

Amulets.
Char.

Caution

One can falter
descending the stairs—
nude or otherwise.

One can be awk-
ward, be conquered,
despair.

One can fall. One can
risk it all, then

regain
balustrades of balance,
palisades of pain.

One can hear
thoughts arise
from the base of the mind.

One can malign
or praise.

The New Hammock

A silver airplane streaks from Italy
to Egypt, to Port Said, across the smoky
blue overlaid with feather-stuffed
white continents around this new
Mediterranean Sea, this quilted
comforter far above me,
its dense warmth the stuff of summer
and bird dreams, while much closer
a grackle streaks across the tops
of trees I've never seen that swish
and bend and toss in a promising wind.

Ascending/Descending

Genesis 28:12

I used to swear I'd never dodder,
twine myself to any nearby plant.

I'd not submit to be fed pudding,
be bathed, be taken to the pot.

I used to say I'd make my exit
well before. How could I have known?

Now I dream, like Jacob, of ladders
into heaven, washed in milk and tears.

In baskets woven of choking vines:
unending fruit and flowers.

Crossing Over

Picking her way through milkweed,
the doe,

haggard, fur stretched
over her bones.

Then
hardly bigger than house cats,

twin fawns—leaping
to take her place.

Transfigured

Up it grew inside her leg,
the bindweed:

a convolution,
a cordage, an intricate rigging

circling bone's blanched trellis,
the sturdy tibia, the condyles
and epicondyles,

the smaller,
tongue-twisting fibula.

There at the knee, an errant vine
coiled behind the meniscus

and sesame seed of patella,
continuing to rise,

knotting
and twining the framework
of pelvis, the comfortable belly.

Then, flowering in the cage
of her bosom—

unfolding, lush—
a flaming blossom.

Acknowledgments

I am grateful to the editors of the following publications in which these poems first appeared, sometimes in different versions:

Alabama Literary Review: "Monarch," "Cornfield Math"
Blue Mesa Review: "My Mother Would Be a Physicist"
Cabinet of Heed: "Infinite Loop"
Conceptions Southwest: "Venus, Cupid, Folly, and Time"
Dual Coast: "What You've Missed So Far"
Dunes Review: "A Toast"
Eunoia Review: "Listen," "Transfigured," "Half-Life," "Love's Last
     Feed," "Obsessions," "Luncheon on the Grass"
Good Works Review: "All My Smoky Aunts," "The Virgin Queen"
Heron Tree: "Some Nights"
Huevos: "The Question"
Indiana Voice Journal: "Ascending, Descending," "Fledgling,"
     "Mercy"
Innisfree Poetry Journal: "Lifted Up," "How It Will Come," "Fable"
Kentucky Review: "Silo and Barn," "In Dad's Old Negatives,"
     "Crossing Over"
Midwest Quarterly: "Aerial View of Seattle, August 1963"
Nixes Mate: "A Short History IV," "Final Deployment"
Northwest Poets & Artists Calendar: "Graveyard Found on Moon"
Peacock Journal: "Afternoon Nap in a Pasture," "Finding Water"
Poetry Northwest: "Lost Things Found"
Prairie Schooner: "Our Lady of the Midnight Kitchen"
Primavera: "Elsewhere"
Red Earth Review: "Dutch Tulip Bubble, 1636-37"
RHINO: "Lost Heart Pond"
The Pennsylvania Review: "Our Father's Garden"
The Southern Review: "Sharing an Artichoke"
Wisconsin Review: "Animals"

About FutureCycle Press

FutureCycle Press is dedicated to publishing English-language poetry books, chapbooks, and anthologies in both print-on-demand and Kindle ebook formats. Founded in 2007 by long-time independent editor/publishers and partners Diane Kistner and Robert S. King, the press incorporated as a nonprofit in 2012. A number of our editors are distinguished poets and writers in their own right, and we have been actively involved in the small press movement going back to the early seventies.

The FutureCycle Poetry Book Prize and honorarium is awarded annually for the best full-length volume of poetry we publish in a calendar year. Introduced in 2013, our Good Works projects are anthologies devoted to issues of universal significance, with all proceeds donated to a related worthy cause. Our Selected Poems series highlights contemporary poets with a substantial body of work to their credit; with this series we strive to resurrect work that has had limited distribution and is now out of print.

We are dedicated to giving all of the authors we publish the care their work deserves, making our catalog of titles the most diverse and distinguished it can be, and paying forward any earnings to fund more great books.

We've learned a few things about independent publishing over the years. We've also evolved a unique, resilient publishing model that allows us to focus mainly on vetting and preserving for posterity poetry collections of exceptional quality without becoming overwhelmed with bookkeeping and mailing, fundraising activities, or taxing editorial and production "bubbles." To find out more about what we are doing, come see us at www.futurecycle.org.

The FutureCycle Poetry Book Prize

All full-length volumes of poetry published by FutureCycle Press in a given calendar year are considered for the annual FutureCycle Poetry Book Prize. This allows us to consider each submission on its own merits, outside of the context of a contest. Too, the judges see the finished book, which will have benefitted from the beautiful book design and strong editorial gloss we are famous for.

The book ranked the best in judging is announced as the prize-winner in the subsequent year. There is no fixed monetary award; instead, the winning poet receives an honorarium of 20% of the total net royalties from all poetry books and chapbooks the press sold online in the year the winning book was published. The winner is also accorded the honor of being on the panel of judges for the next year's competition; all judges receive copies of all contending books to keep for their personal library.

www.ingramcontent.com/pod-product-compliance
Lightning Source LLC
Chambersburg PA
CBHW070008100426
42741CB00012B/3156